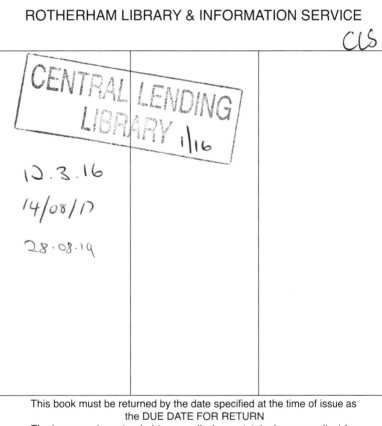

DANGEROUS DINOSAURS

SEA MONSTERS

Liz Miles

W
FRANKLIN WATTS
LONDON · SYDNEY

First published in 2015 by Franklin Watts

Copyright © Arcturus Holdings Limited

Franklin Watts
338 Euston Road
London
NW1 3BH

Franklin Watts Australia
Level 17/207 Kent Street, Sydney, NSW 2000

Produced by Arcturus Publishing Limited,
26/27 Bickels Yard, 151–153 Bermondsey Street, London SE1 3HA

The right of Liz Miles to be identified as the author of this work has
been asserted by her in accordance with the Copyright, Designs and
Patents Act 1988.

Author: Liz Miles
Editors: Joe Harris, Alex Woolf and Joe Fullman
Designer: Emma Randall
Original design concept: Notion Design

Picture Credits:
Key: b-bottom, m-middle, l-left, r-right, t-top
All images by pixel-shack.com except for:
Shutterstock: p10 b, p21 b, p24 t, p24 b, p25 t, p25 m, p25 b.
Wikipedia Commons: p17 b.

A CIP catalogue record for this book is available from the British Library.

Dewey Decimal Classification Number: 567.9'12-dc23
ISBN: 978 1 4451 4161 9

Printed in China

Franklin Watts is a division of Hachette Children's Books, an Hachette
UK company.
www.hachette.co.uk

SL004436UK

Supplier 03, Date 1214, Print Run 3762

CONTENTS

FROM THE DEEP

Some of the deadliest and weirdest-looking creatures that ever lived swam in prehistoric seas. There were armoured fish, fearsome 'sea lizards' such as Tylosaurus (TIE-low-SORE-us), huge turtles, terrifying sharks, fish-like lizards called ichthyosaurs (ICK-thee-oh-sores) and long-necked creatures called plesiosaurs (PLEH-see-oh-sores).

Tylosaurus, the predator shown above, was a fast-swimming mosasaur (MOE-za-sore). It was a fearsome killer, easily devouring the largest of prey, such as giant turtles and sharks. Tylosaurus may also have fed on dinosaur flesh, because Tylosaurus teeth marks have been found on the body of a duck-billed dinosaur called a hadrosaur (HA-dro-sore).

GIANTS OF THE OCEAN

The prehistoric ocean contained super-sized versions of creatures familiar to us today. For example, Archelon (ARE-kell-on) was the biggest turtle ever known. About 4 m (13 ft) long and the weight of a family car, it had a leathery shell. It snapped up prey such as jellyfish and shelled creatures using its powerful, sharp-edged beak. Archelon may have lived for up to 100 years, and some scientists think it hibernated on the ocean floor.

SHELL SHOCK

Prehistoric seas were teeming with weird-looking shelled creatures. The most well-known are trilobites (TRY-low-bites) and ammonites (AM-mow-nites). That's because fossils of their exoskeletons are so common.

Ammonites had spiral-shaped shells that could grow to huge sizes. Many of them, such as Oxynoticeras (OCKS-ee-NOT-i-SEER-us), were good swimmers, while others were slow-swimming bottom dwellers. They may have avoided predators by squirting ink, like today's octopuses and squid.

FLOATING AIDS

The ammonite's shell was strong enough to allow it to swim to great depths without being crushed by the pressure of the water. The inner chambers could be filled with gas to help the ammonite float upward when it wanted to rise.

BIG SOFTY

Just inside the entrance of this coiled shell lurked the soft body of a Hildoceras (HIL-doh-SEER-us) ammonite. It squirted jets of water from its body to whizz through the water, often moving around with others in large schools in search of food.

SQUASHING JAWS

Tentacles reached out to catch its food and then draw it up into its hidden mouth. It is believed that this creature survived on microscopic organisms called plankton.

DEEP SEA ROACHES

The trilobites survived for more than 270 million years, scavenging, hunting and filter-feeding on the ocean floor. There were many types of trilobite, now all extinct, but they are all related to the cockroaches and millipedes of today. They shed their protective exoskeleton several times as they got bigger, and a new one would grow in its place. Groups of up to 1,000 swarmed together so they could stay safe while waiting for their new shell to develop. Faced with danger, they curled up to keep their softer underbodies safe.

VITAL STATISTICS

AMMONITES

Meaning of name: Named after the Egyptian god Ammon

Family: Hildoceratidae

Period: Devonian to Cretaceous

Size: Up to 2 m (6.5 ft) diameter

Weight: 5-10 kg / 11-22 lb

Diet: Plankton

The spiral shell of the ammonite was divided into individual chambers. The creature lived in the largest, outermost of these chambers. When it became too big for a chamber, it grew another one and moved in there. Scientists estimate that it took about four weeks to grow a chamber, so they could grow around 13 per year. You can work out the age of an ammonite by counting the chambers in its shell.

CAMEROCERAS

TENTACLED TERROR

If you went for a swim in the seas of the Ordovician period, you might have encountered a spine-chilling Cameroceras (CAM-ur-oh-SEER-us). This massive squid-like monster may have been up to 9 m (30 ft) in length. It was the largest mollusk (soft-bodied invertebrate) ever known, and a top predator.

HUGE HORN

This creature's horn-shaped shell was made up of separated chambers, like an ammonite's. Its name means 'chambered horn'. As the animal grew, the shell grew to fit its increasing size. The animal lived in the top third of the shell, closest to the opening, so that it could reach out and grab its prey. Gas filled the shell chambers behind to help the creature move up and down in the seas.

FISH FEEDER

Cameroceras probably fed on any prey that came within the reach of its terrifying tentacles, such as the jawless fish that lived in the seas at that time.

A CANNIBAL?

Cameroceras is sometimes illustrated as a cannibal, eating its young. Scientists cannot be sure of their diet or how they hunted. Only their shells are found as fossils – all evidence of their soft bodies rotted away, leaving no lasting clues, such as stomach contents.

A TIGHT GRIP

Cameroceras had many long tentacles with sticky hooks, which it used to trap its prey.

TRACKING PREY

Like today's squid, Cameroceras may have tracked down its prey by picking up scents, or by using its simple pinhole eyes. Because it was so large, it may have stayed on the ocean floor, lying in wait to ambush passing creatures. Once spotted, the meal would be snatched, held firmly, then pulled into its horny, beak-like mouth. There would have been little chance of escape.

THEN AND NOW

Estimates of the size of Cameroceras are based on a fossil of part of its shell. Scientists can guess at how it lived by studying related species that exist today, such as cuttlefish, octopus and squid (such as this one).

SUPER-SHARKS

Just as today, sharks were the greatest terrors of the seas in prehistory. But back then, sharks were even larger and deadlier. Weighing up to 100 tonnes (110 tons), Megalodon (MEG-ah-low-don) prowled the seas after the dinosaurs had died out and is the largest marine predator in the history of the planet.

Megalodon was longer than a school bus – that's three times longer than today's great white shark. Its teeth were over 15 cm (6 in) long and among the biggest choppers in the prehistoric world. Not only that, Megalodon had the most powerful bite of any creature that ever lived, with a bite force of 11–18 tonnes (12–20 tons) – enough to crush the skull of a whale.

SEA CREATURE DETECTIVES

Fossil teeth from prehistoric sharks were thought at first to be tongues because they were so big. A Megalodon tooth, such as this one, was similar to a great white's – triangular, sharp and serrated. The serrations acted like the grooves in a saw, cutting through flesh as the shark shook its prey from side to side.

NO ESCAPE

Large fins allow for speedy turns, so Megalodon was an agile hunter. It may have chased whales to the surface when they needed to take a breath. The shark would attack from below and perhaps bite into the whale's underbelly before it could escape.

GIANT OF THE OCEANS

Megalodon's body is estimated to have been up to 20 m (65 ft) in length. From 25 to 1.6 million years ago, there was no ocean creature strong enough to compete with this monster shark.

KING-SIZE BITE

Megalodon's jaws were so vast a person would be able to stand up in its wide-open mouth. Its bite was so powerful that once it had a part of its prey in its mouth, like a fin, it would have been virtually impossible to escape. With an enormous hunger and a bite this size, huge whales would have been its target prey.

DINOSAUR BITES

Squalicorax (SKWA-lih-COR-ax) was a sharp-toothed shark that terrorised Cretaceous seas, feeding on smaller creatures like Enchodus (EN-coe-duss), a type of prehistoric fish. The foot bone of a hadrosaur was found with a Squalicorax tooth in it, suggesting that the shark was happy to turn scavenger and feed on a dead dinosaur that had been washed into the sea.

LONG-NECKED HUNTERS

The plesiosaurs were ferocious aquatic reptiles. They had to surface regularly to breathe air, just like modern whales and dolphins. Among the strangest looking plesiosaurs were the elasmosaurs (el-LAZZ-moe-sores), which had very long necks and lived in Cretaceous waters. Their small heads were packed with sharp teeth that snatched up even the fastest-swimming prey.

WEIGHTY BELLY
Elasmosaurs, like other plesiosaurs, ate stones. These are called gastroliths. Their weight may have helped their barrel-like bodies to stay stable.

BELLY STONES

We know that elasmosaurs ate stones because they have been found in fossils of these creatures. Gastroliths may have helped with digestion because as the elasmosaurs moved, the stones knocked against and mashed up the food they had eaten.

PADDLE POWER
Although elasmosaurs look ungainly, they were able to move their bodies up and down in a wave-like motion, similar to a swimming penguin, and flap their stiff paddles as if flying through the ocean. The front paddles were used for steering while the back ones produced the force to push their enormous bodies slowly through the water.

VITAL STATISTICS

Meaning of name:
Ribbon lizard

Family: Elasmosauridae

Period: Late Cretaceous

Size: 12 m (40 ft) long

Weight:
2,000 kg / 2 tons

Diet: Fish

STICK YOUR NECK OUT

Albertonectes (al-BER-to-NEK-teez),
a type of elasmosaur, had a neck 7 m
(23 ft) in length – longer than any other
known plesiosaur. It had 76 neck vertebrae,
while mammals, including giraffes, only
have seven. Such a long neck enabled it to
grasp prey without having to swim far.

SNEAKY EATERS

The neck of Elasmosaurus, a type of elasmosaur, was so long
that, at first, scientists thought its neck fossils were part of a
tail. Elasmosaurus's long neck and small head were perfect
for sneaking up on schools of fish to eat. Elasmosaurus
reached out for fish, while keeping its bulky body well-
hidden in deeper, murky waters. The long, thin teeth that
stuck out from its mouth were like skewers.

LIOPLEURODON

JURASSIC TYRANT

Liopleurodon (LIE-oh-PLOOR-oh-don) is among the largest flesh-eating vertebrates ever to have lived. It was a short-necked plesiosaur – a voracious meat-eater and top hunter, which prowled the Jurassic seas for fish and other marine life, such as ichthyosaurs (ICK-thee-oh-sores) and squid.

The position of Liopleurodon's nostrils suggest that they were used for smelling, not breathing. The predator probably used its sense of smell to find its next meal, perhaps picking up on the presence of flesh or blood from long distances away. Its four powerful paddles would have given it a good chance of winning a chase, and its quick acceleration would have been ideal for ambushing prey.

TERRIFIC TEETH

With teeth the size of a T. rex's, Liopleurodon could take deadly bites, snapping at flesh or grabbing fish whole. Some of its teeth were 20 cm (8 inches) in length – the size of bananas – and stuck out at the front like a vicious animal trap. The huge head was a fifth of its body length and contained jaws powerful enough to hold onto a struggling Ichthyosaurus. Some experts believe it swam with its mouth open, catching any fish or squid that happened across its path.

LIOPLEURODON
VERSUS
TYRANNOSAURUS REX

	LIOPLEURODON	TYRANNOSAURUS REX
LENGTH	18 m / 59 ft	12 m / 39 ft
WEIGHT	25 tons	7.7 tons
JAW LENGTH	Over 3 m (9.8 ft)	1.2 m (4 ft)
PREY	Fish and other marine life	Meat
PERIOD	Mid-Late Jurassic	Late Cretaceous

MASSIVE-JAWED MONSTERS

The pliosaurs (PLY-oh-sores) were plesiosaurs with short necks, large heads and massive, toothed jaws. They ranged from 4 to 15 m (13–49 ft) in length and preyed on fish, sharks, dinosaurs and other marine reptiles.

TITAN OF THE SEA

Among the largest pliosaurs was Kronosaurus (crow-no-SORE-us). Named after the Greek titan Kronos, its big head, sturdy neck and sharp teeth evoke the terrifying power of a mythical giant. Its huge, flat-topped skull made up a third of its body length and is bigger than the skull of any other known marine reptile. The pointed jaws hid rounded but deadly back teeth that could crush the shells of ammonites and turtles.

MUSCLE BOUND

There is evidence that Kronosaurus had strong muscles for swimming, so it was probably fast and agile in the water in spite of its bulky body.

DINO HUNTERS?

Pliosaurus (PLY-oh-SORE-us) was another giant pliosaur. Scientists estimate that its jaws would have been able to bite together with more force than those of a T. rex. The size of its teeth and the power of its jaws suggest that it may have had the strength to grab dinosaurs from the shore and devour them. Dinosaur bones have certainly been found in the stomachs of Pliosauruses. However, these may have come from rotting dinosaur corpses, carried by the tide or a river into the ocean.

SEA MONSTER DETECTIVES

Sometimes only a few parts of a sea monster are discovered. Working out which part belongs where can be a bit like doing a jigsaw puzzle. Another challenge is classifying these creatures. This image shows a Trinacromerum (TRY-nack-roe-MARE-um), a type of plesiosaur – but it was originally mistaken for another, similar-looking species of plesiosaur called a Dolichorhynchops (DOE-lih-co-RIN-cops).

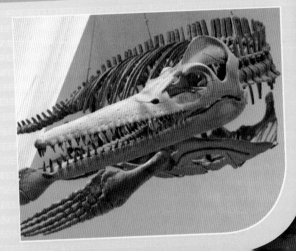

ICHTHYOSAURS

FISH-LIZARDS

The ichthyosaurs (ICK-thee-oh-sores), or 'fish-lizards', looked a little like dolphins, but they were reptiles rather than mammals. These deadly hunters of Jurassic times boasted a fearsome set of jaws.

Ichthyosaurs like Ichthyosaurus (ICK-thee-oh-SORE-us) and Excalibosaurus (ex-CAL-ih-bo-SORE-us) were awesome swimmers and well adapted to hunt for prey, or scavenge if necessary.

SHARK-LIKE HUNTERS

The 2 m (6.6 ft) long Ichthyosaurus had a dolphin-shaped body but its tail looked more like a shark's. It also lived like a shark, hunting in deep, open waters. The long, tooth-filled jaws snapped up shellfish, fish and squid.

BEADY EYES

Ichthyosaurus's eyes were extra large to help pick up what light they could in the murky ocean depths.

HUNTING SPEED

Two sets of flippers and a dorsal fin stabilised the Ichthyosaurus as it swam. It propelled itself through the water with flicks of its tail, moving quickly thanks to its body's streamlined shape.

SWORD-LIP

Some ichthyosaurs, such as Excalibosaurus, had a longer, sword-like upper jaw. Excalibosaurus is named after Excalibur, King Arthur's mythical weapon. Its 'sword' might have been used as a probe to dig for food on the ocean floor. Or it may have been used as a weapon in battles or to capture its prey. The part of the top jaw that extended beyond the lower jaw was lined with rows of outward-facing teeth, which would have been deadly if stabbed into the flesh of its prey or an enemy reptile.

EXCALIBOSAURUS VERSUS SWORDFISH

	EXCALIBOSAURUS	SWORDFISH
LENGTH	7 m / 23 ft	3 m / 9.8 ft
WEIGHT	907 kg / 2,000 lb	650 kg / 1,430 lb
TEETH	On upper and lower jaw	No teeth in adults
PREY	Fish, other marine life and reptiles	Fish, squid, octopus
PERIOD	Late Jurassic	Now

FEARSOME FISH

Sharks were not the only deadly prehistoric fish. Some ancient fish, such as the huge Dunkleosteus (DUNK-lee-owe-STEE-us), were easily powerful enough to attack and kill a shark. Other predatory fish, such as Enchodus (EN-coe-duss), make today's piranhas look positively friendly.

WELL PROTECTED
Dunkleosteus had tough protective plating to shield its enormous 10-m (33-ft) long, 3-tonne (3.3-ton) body against other hunters in the Devonian seas. Bite marks on these fish suggest that they sometimes turned to cannibalism when other food was hard to find.

MEAT SLICERS
Instead of teeth, Dunkleosteus had slicing, bony plates. It bit hard with one part of its jaw, capturing even powerful, struggling prey.

JAWS!
Dunkleosteus had a greater biting force than a great white shark. Its bone-crushing jaws had a force of 500 kg (1100 lbs) – more than twice as powerful as a hyena's.

SHARP-TOOTHED KILLERS

Enchodus, which lived in the Late Cretaceous, could almost be mistaken for a modern salmon or herring – except for its mouthful of huge, sharp teeth. At the front of its mouth were two piercing fangs that could grow up to 6 cm (2.4 in) in length. These fangs, together with its large eyes, made it a formidable hunter. Like many types of fish, it might have lived and hunted in schools. A group of these fang-mouthed monsters could have overcome marine creatures far bigger than themselves.

SEA MONSTER DETECTIVES

Three-dimensional computer models of extinct monsters like Dunkleosteus are created to discover more about how they moved and hunted. A computer model of Dunkleosteus revealed that it could open its jaws in just a fiftieth of a second – fast enough to have created a suction force capable of pulling passing prey into its mouth.

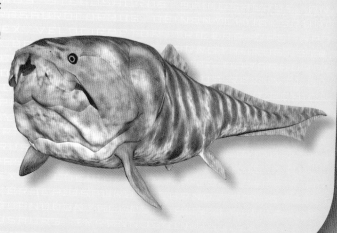

GIANT CROCS

Cretaceous swamps, lakes, rivers and estuaries were dangerous places for small land animals to wander. Even huge dinosaurs were at risk of a surprise attack from one of the giant crocodiles that lurked there. Bite marks on dinosaurs, including the massive carnivore Albertosaurus, reveal attacks from Deinosuchus (DIE-no-SOO-kuss), one of the biggest crocodiles to exist.

Prehistoric crocodiles were probably even more terrifying than modern-day crocs. Gigantic creatures like the 'supercroc' Sarcosuchus (sar-co-SOOK-us) and Deinosuchus (which means 'terrible crocodile') hid in shallow waters, waiting to ambush their prey.

HORRIFIC!

Deinosuchus had huge jaws with about 44 sharp teeth, and it had a horrific bite, more powerful than some of the biggest dinosaurs. With a 10-m (33-ft) long body, and a skull longer than an adult human is tall, this monster must have had quite an appetite, so a large dinosaur was probably a tempting meal. It lived in river mouths, where it also snapped up turtles and fish.

SUPERCROC

The length of a bus and the weight of a small whale, Sarcosuchus, nicknamed 'supercroc', was the biggest crocodile-like creature ever known, and twice the size of any crocodile living today. Its teeth were rounded, and built for grabbing at prey and crushing, not for taking bites. It probably lay half-submerged in shallow rivers, dining on large fish and any other prey that wandered by. It may also have crawled onto land to tuck into the remains of carrion, left over from a dinosaur kill. Sarcosuchus had a peculiar bulbous tip at the end of its snout, called a bulla. Scientists don't know what this was for, but it may have helped it make sounds, or enhanced its sense of smell.

SARCOSUCHUS

VITAL STATISTICS

Meaning of name:
Flesh crocodile

Family: Pholidosauridae

Period: Early Cretaceous

Size: 12 m (40 ft) long

Weight: 9,000-13,600 kg / 10-15 tons

Diet: Fish and carrion

CHANGING SEAS

About 65 million years ago, life on Earth was transformed by a catastrophe that wiped out the dinosaurs and caused the extinction of many species of sea creatures. Most scientists believe that this mass death was caused by a large asteroid hitting the Earth. Some argue that volcanoes also played a crucial part in the extinction.

LEGENDS

Did the long-necked plesiosaurs really die out completely at the end of the Age of the Dinosaurs? Some authors have argued that a small number have survived to the present day. They believe that they can be found in places such as Loch Ness, in Scotland. While this is an exciting idea, there is very little evidence to support the theory.

ARMAGEDDON

The extinction event at the end of the Cretaceous period brought an end to nearly three-quarters of ocean species, including giants such as Tylosaurus.

CHAIN REACTION

After the meteor crashed into the Earth, a huge amount of smoke and dust was thrown into the air. This had the effect of blocking out the sun. Ocean plant-life died off, because there was no longer enough sunlight to sustain it. The death of so many plants caused a chain reaction. Plant-eating sea creatures died from lack of food, and then the predators that ate them were affected too.

AFTER THE MONSTERS

After the disappearance of the large sea reptiles such as mosasaurs and plesiosaurs, other creatures took their place at the top of the food chain. Sharks became the undisputed top dogs of the oceans – a position they still hold today.

 # SEA MONSTER DETECTIVES

By looking at fossils, we can tell that some creatures in today's oceans have hardly changed since prehistoric times. Horseshoe crabs are often described as 'living fossils' because they are almost identical to creatures that lived 450 million years ago – before even the dinosaurs evolved. Other creatures that have changed very little include sharks.

FOSSIL FINDS

Sea monster fossils form at the bottom of the ocean, but over millions of years the rocks change position and some become part of the land. The map shows some examples of important finds.

ELASMOSAURUS

FOUND IN: North America
Fossils of a long-necked plesiosaur were given the name Elasmosaurus in 1868, after their discovery in Kansas in the USA.

SARCOSUCHUS

FOUND IN: Africa/South America
Fossils from this 'supercroc' were first found in the 1940s in Algeria and, later, Niger – including a complete skull in 1964. Fossils of teeth and other bones from Brazil have also been identified as the supercroc's.

MEGALODON

FOUND: Worldwide
People have been finding fossil teeth of Megalodon for hundreds of years worldwide. At first they were thought to be dragons' teeth. Later they were identified as belonging to this massive prehistoric shark.

KRONOSAURUS

FOUND IN: Australia, South America
Kronosaurus fossils have been found in Australia and Colombia. The first Kronosaurus fossil (part of a skull) was found in 1899 but it took additional fossils and 25 more years to name the creature.

PLIOSAURUS
FOUND IN: Europe
A skeleton from a new species of Pliosaurus was found on the Norwegian island of Spitsbergen in 2006, but it took many years and more discoveries to name the predator. Until it could be properly identified, the deadly hunter was nicknamed Predator X by scientists.

LIOPLEURODON
FOUND IN: Europe
The first Liopleurodon fossils were three teeth found in France, and the creature was named in 1873. Liopleurodon fossils have since been found mainly in France and England.

CAMEROCERAS
FOUND IN: Europe, North America, China
Fossils of this giant tentacled mollusc, first named in 1842, have been found all around the world in sediments that used to be ocean beds.

Prehistoric sea creatures came in all sizes, many of them far bigger than a modern-day killer whale.

Dinosaur Size Guide
- Killer whale – 6 m (20 ft)
- Cameroceras – 9 m (30 ft)
- Elasmosaurus – 12 m (40 ft)
- Liopleurodon – 18 m (59 ft)
- Megalodon – 20 m (65 ft)

TIMELINE

OF LIFE ON EARTH

Scientists have divided the billions of years of prehistoric time into periods. Dinosaurs lived in the Triassic, Cretaceous and Jurassic periods, while modern humans evolved in the Quaternary period.

← CAMBRIAN
541–485 mya: Life forms become more complex.

↓ SILURIAN
443–419 mya: First creatures on land.

↑ ORDOVICIAN
485–443 mya: Arthropods (creatures with exoskeletons) rule the seas. Plants colonise the land.

↑ PRECAMBRIAN
4,570–541 million years ago (mya): The first life forms appear. They are tiny, one-celled creatures.

↑ DEVONIAN
419–359 mya: First insects evolve. Fish now dominate the seas.

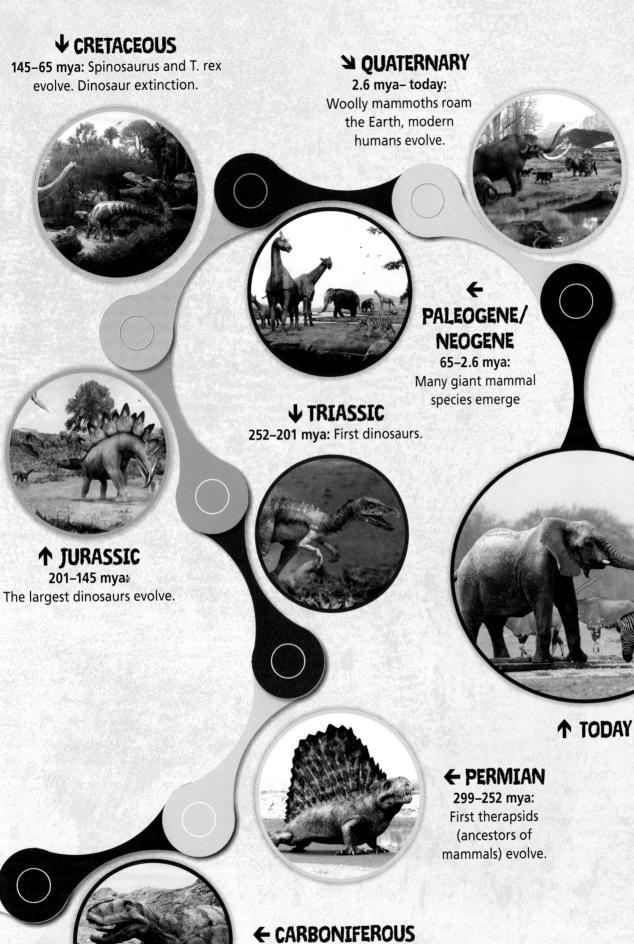

↓ CRETACEOUS
145–65 mya: Spinosaurus and T. rex evolve. Dinosaur extinction.

↘ QUATERNARY
2.6 mya– today: Woolly mammoths roam the Earth, modern humans evolve.

← PALEOGENE/ NEOGENE
65–2.6 mya: Many giant mammal species emerge

↓ TRIASSIC
252–201 mya: First dinosaurs.

↑ JURASSIC
201–145 mya: The largest dinosaurs evolve.

↑ TODAY

← PERMIAN
299–252 mya: First therapsids (ancestors of mammals) evolve.

← CARBONIFEROUS
359–299 mya: Reptiles first appear, vast forests cover the land.

29

GLOSSARY

Carboniferous A prehistoric period when there were many swamps and forests.

carrion Flesh from a creature that has died, and a source of food for some animals.

Cretaceous A prehistoric period during which mammals and dinosaurs lived. It ended with the mass extinction of the dinosaurs 65 million years ago.

Devonian A prehistoric period when the oceans were warm and filled with many types of evolving fish.

dorsal fin An upright flipper rising up from the back of a fish and used for steering and stability.

evolve To change gradually over time.

extinct Not existing anymore.

filter-feeding Feeding by filtering out nutrients or plankton floating in the water.

flippers Limbs used by creatures in the water for swimming.

food chain A group of organisms arranged in order of rank, with each dependent on the next as a source of food. For example, a fox eats a mouse, the mouse eats an insect, and the insect eats a plant.

fossil The remains of a prehistoric organism preserved in rock.

fossilised Made into a fossil.

hadrosaurs Plant-eating family of dinosaurs, also known as duck-billed dinosaurs because of their beak-like mouths.

hibernating Spending the winter in a dormant (slowed-down or inactive) state.

ichthyosaurs A group of large, sea-living reptiles that looked similar to dolphins.

invertebrate A creature without a backbone, such as a worm, a squid, or an insect.

Jurassic A prehistoric period in which many large dinosaurs lived.

mosasaur A giant, meat-eating, and sea-living family of reptiles that used four paddle-like limbs to swim.

prey An animal that is hunted by other animals for food.

reptiles Cold-blooded animals that usually lay eggs and have scales.

streamlined Something that is smoothly shaped, enabling it to move easily through water.

Triassic A prehistoric period during which the first dinosaurs and mammals evolved.

vertebrate A creature with a backbone, such as a bird, mammal, or reptile.

FURTHER INFORMATION

FURTHER READING

Dinosaur Record Breakers by Darren Naish (Carlton Kids, 2014)

Dinosaurs: A Children's Encyclopedia by editors of DK (Dorling Kindersley, 2011)

Evolution Revolution by Robert Winston (Dorling Kindersley, 2009)

National Geographic Kids: The Ultimate Dinopedia by Don Lessem
(National Geographic Society, 2012)

Prehistoric Safari: Sea Monsters by Liz Miles (Franklin Watts, 2012)

The Usborne World Atlas of Dinosaurs by Susanna Davidson
(Usborne Publishing, 2013)

WEBSITES

http://www.bbc.co.uk/nature/14343366
A regularly updated part of the BBC website, dedicated to dinosaurs.
There is a news section and plenty of cool videos.

http://animals.nationalgeographic.com/animals/prehistoric/
This part of the National Geographic website is home to some fascinating articles
about dinosaurs. There are also some excellent pictures.

www.nhm.ac.uk/kids-only/index.html
The young people's section of the Natural History Museum website. Packed
with downloads, games, quizzes and lots of information about dinosaurs.

INDEX

SERIES CONTENTS

DINOSAUR DEFENDERS
Attack and Defence • Triceratops: Horn-Faced Fighter • Frightening Frills • Pachycephalosaurids: Butting Boneheads • Stegosaurus: Savage Spiker • Ankylosaurs: Defensive Demons • Hadrosaurs: Deafening Duckbills • Sauropods: Tail-Thrashing Titans • Patterns and Feathers • Herding Heavies • Danger Senses • Dino World • Timeline of Life on Earth

DINOSAUR RECORD-BREAKERS
Battling Giants • Titanosaurs: The Heavyweights • Smallest Dinosaurs • Ultimate Hunter: Spinosaurus • Deadliest Dinosaur • Skyscrapers • Dinosaur Egg Records • Fastest Dinosaurs • Longest Claws • Tough as Tanks: Best Protection • Smart Cookies or Bird Brains? • Famous Fossils • Timeline of Life on Earth

DINOSAURS AND THE PREHISTORIC WORLD
Dinosaur Planet • Changing Earth • Timeline of Life on Earth • Underwater Creatures • Emerging onto the Land • Early Reptiles: Fierce Forerunners • The First Dinosaurs: Hungry Hunters • Age of the Dinosaurs • Dino Diets • Extinction Event • After the Dinosaurs: Savage Mammals • Descendants of the Dinosaurs • Dino World

KILLER DINOSAURS
Ultimate Predators • Tyrant Lizard • Ravenous Giant • Utahraptor: Vicious Pack Hunter • Sickle-Clawed Runners • Carnotaurus: 'Flesh-Eating Bull' • Troodon: Night Tracker • Terrifying Teeth • Baryonyx: Fish Hunter • Packs and Families • Savage Killers or Just Scavengers? • Dino World • Timeline of Life on Earth

FLYING MONSTERS
Savage Skies • Needle-Toothed Terrors • Pteranodons: Awesome Axe-Heads • Jutting-Jawed Pterosaurs • Dimorphodon: Tooth-Beaked Hunter • Furry Fiends • Quetzalcoatlus: Giant Vulture • Crested Competitors • Keen Eyed Killers • Bird-Like Biters • Flying Families • Winged World • Timeline of Life on Earth

SEA MONSTERS
From the Deep • Shell Shock • Cameroceras: Tentacled Terror • Super-Sharks • Long-Necked Hunters • Liopleurodon: Jurassic Tyrant • Massive-Jawed Monsters • Ichthyosaurs: Fish-Lizards • Fearsome Fish • Giant Crocs • Changing Seas • Fossil Finds • Timeline of Life on Earth